Edward Augustus Freeman

The historical Geography of Europe

Vol. 2

Edward Augustus Freeman

The historical Geography of Europe
Vol. 2

ISBN/EAN: 9783743349643

Manufactured in Europe, USA, Canada, Australia, Japa

Cover: Foto ©ninafisch / pixelio.de

Manufactured and distributed by brebook publishing software (www.brebook.com)

Edward Augustus Freeman

The historical Geography of Europe

HISTORICAL GEOGRAPHY

OF

EUROPE

BY

EDWARD A. FREEMAN, D.C.L., LL.D.

HONORARY FELLOW OF TRINITY COLLEGE, OXFORD

IN TWO VOLUMES

VOL. II.—MAPS

SECOND EDITION

LONDON
LONGMANS, GREEN, AND CO.
NEW YORK
SCRIBNER AND WELFORD
1882

LIST OF MAPS.

Nos.
- I. HOMERIC GREECE AND THE NEIGHBOURING LANDS.
- II. GREECE AND THE GREEK COLONIES.
- III. GREECE IN THE FIFTH CENTURY B.C.
- IV. THE LANDS ROUND THE ÆGÆAN AT THE BEGINNING OF THE KLEOMENIC WAR.
- V. DOMINIONS AND DEPENDENCIES OF ALEXANDER. *circa* B.C. 323.
- VI. KINGDOMS OF THE SUCCESSORS OF ALEXANDER, c. B.C. 300.
- VII. ITALY BEFORE THE GROWTH OF THE ROMAN POWER.
- VIII. THE MEDITERRANEAN LANDS AT THE BEGINNING OF THE SECOND PUNIC WAR.
- IX. THE ROMAN DOMINIONS AT THE END OF THE MITHRIDATIC WAR, B.C. 64.
- X. THE ROMAN EMPIRE AT THE DEATH OF AUGUSTUS, A.D. 13.
- XI. THE ROMAN EMPIRE UNDER TRAJAN, A.D. 117.
- XII. THE ROMAN EMPIRE DIVIDED INTO PREFECTURES.

LIST OF MAPS.

Nos.		
XIII.	EUROPE IN THE REIGN OF THEODORIC, c. A.D. 500.	
XIV.	EUROPE AT THE DEATH OF JUSTINIAN, A.D. 565.	
XV.	EUROPE END OF SEVENTH CENTURY, A.D. 695.	
XVI.	GREATEST EXTENT OF THE SARACEN DOMINIONS.	
XVII.	EUROPE IN THE TIME OF CHARLES THE GREAT, A.D. 814.	
XVIII.	THE WESTERN EMPIRE AS DIVIDED AT VERDUN, A.D. 843.	
XIX.	THE WESTERN EMPIRE AS DIVIDED A.D. 870.	
XX.	DITTO DITTO	A.D. 887.
XXI.	CENTRAL EUROPE, c. A.D. 980.	
XXII.	CENTRAL EUROPE, A.D. 1180.	
XXIII.	DITTO	A.D. 1360.
XXIV.	DITTO	A.D. 1460.
XXV.	DITTO	A.D. 1555.
XXVI.	DITTO	A.D. 1660.
XXVII.	DITTO	A.D. 1780.
XXVIII.	DITTO	A.D. 1801.
XXIX.	DITTO	A.D. 1810.
XXX.	DITTO	A.D. 1815.
XXXI.	DITTO	A.D. 1860.
XXXII.	DITTO	A.D. 1871.

LIST OF MAPS.

XXXIII.	BOUNDARIES OF FRANCE, A.D. 1555, 1715, 1791, 1871		
XXXIV.	SOUTH-EASTERN EUROPE, c. A.D. 910.		
XXXV.	DITTO	DITTO	c. A.D. 1000.
XXXVI.	DITTO	DITTO	c. A.D. 1040–1070.
XXXVII.	DITTO	DITTO	c. A.D. 1105.
XXXVIII.	DITTO	DITTO	c. A.D. 1180.
XXXIX.	DITTO	DITTO	c. A.D. 1210.
XL.	DITTO	DITTO	c. A.D. 1340.
XLI.	DITTO	DITTO	c. A.D. 1354–1358.
XLII.	DITTO	DITTO	c. A.D. 1401.
XLIII.	DITTO	DITTO	c. A.D. 1444.
XLIV.	DITTO	DITTO	c. A.D. 1464.
XLV.	DITTO	DITTO	c. A.D. 1672.
XLVI.	DITTO	DITTO	c. A.D. 1700.
XLVII.	DITTO	DITTO	c. A.D. 1727.
XLVIII.	SOUTH-EASTERN EUROPE, A.D. 1864.		
XLIX.	SOUTH-EASTERN EUROPE, ACCORDING TO THE TREATY OF BERLIN, A.D. 1878.		
L.	THE BALTIC LANDS, c. A.D. 1000.		
LI.	DITTO	c. A.D. 1220.	
LII.	DITTO	c. A.D. 1270.	

LIST OF MAPS.

Nos.
LIII. THE BALTIC LANDS, c. A.D. 1350-60.
LIV. DITTO c. A.D. 1400.
LV. DITTO c. A.D. 1478.
LVI. DITTO c. A.D. 1563.
LVII. DITTO c. A.D. 1617.
LVIII. DITTO c. A.D. 1701.
LIX. DITTO c. A.D. 1772.
LX. DITTO c. A.D. 1795.
LXI. DITTO c. A.D. 1809.
LXII. THE SPANISH KINGDOMS, A.D. 1030.
LXIII. DITTO DITTO A.D. 1210.
LXIV. DITTO DITTO A.D. 1360.
LXV. THE SPANISH KINGDOMS, AND THEIR EUROPEAN DEPENDENCIES UNDER CHARLES THE FIFTH.

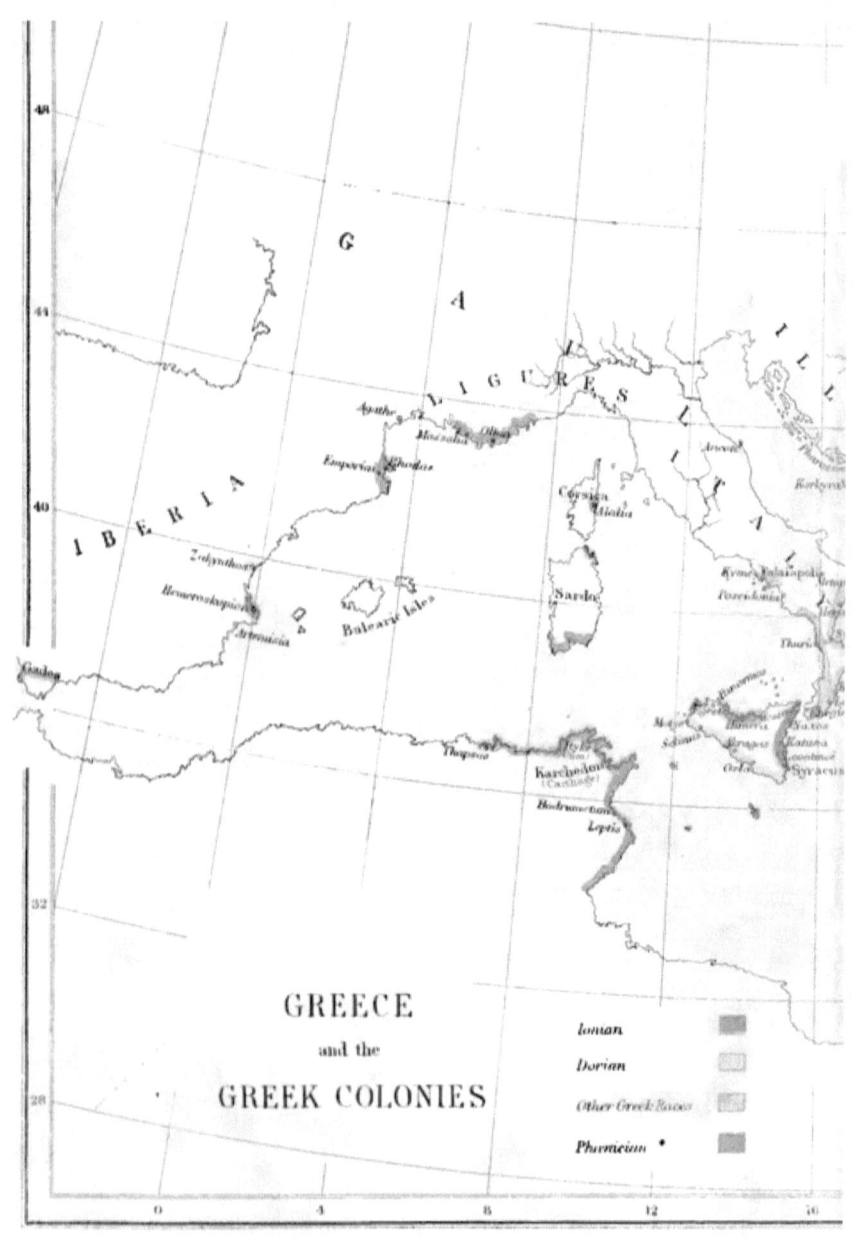

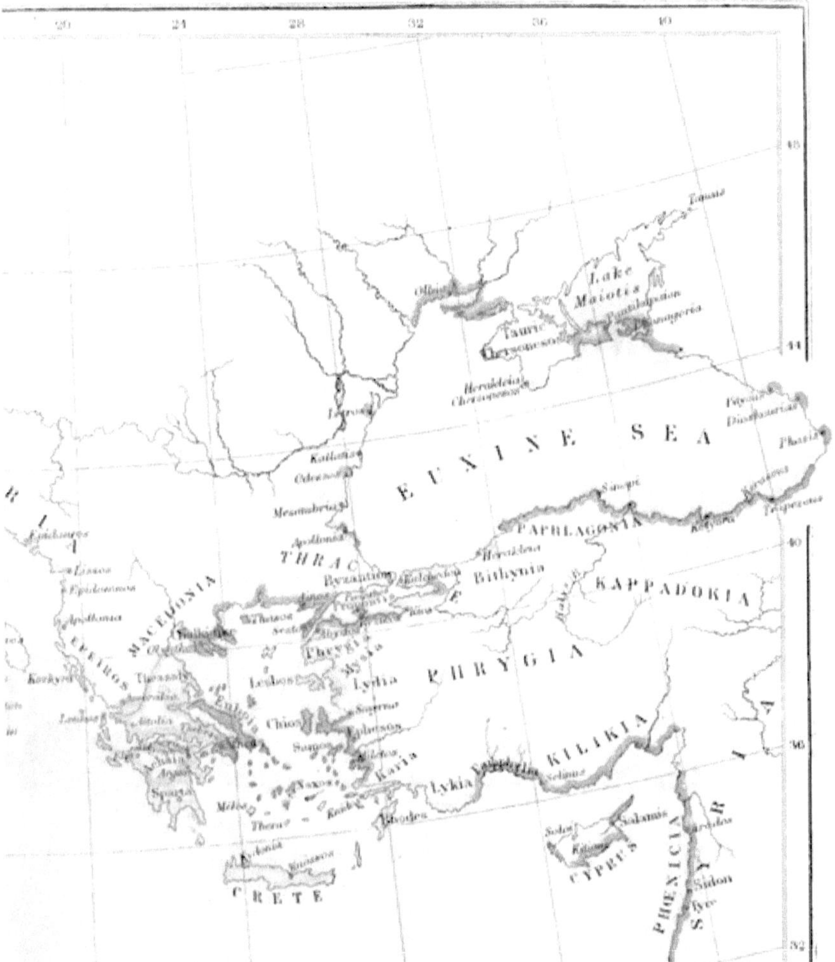
EUXINE SEA
Lake Maiotis
Tanais
Pantikapaion
Phanagoria
Tauric Chersonesos
Olbia
Istros
Kallatis
Odessos
Mesembria
Apollonia
THRACE
Byzantium
Kalchedon
Herakleia
Bithynia
PAPHLAGONIA
Sinope
Phasis
Trapezous
KAPPADOKIA
PHRYGIA
MACEDONIA
EPEIROS
Korkyra
Thasos
Sestos
Lesbos
Chios
Samos
Smyrna
Ephesos
Miletos
Karia
Lydia
Mysia
Lykia
KILIKIA
Naxos
Melos
Thera
Rhodes
CRETE
Knossos
Salamis
CYPRUS
PHOENICIA
Sidon
SYRIA
Kyrene
Barka
Kyrenaica
EGYPT

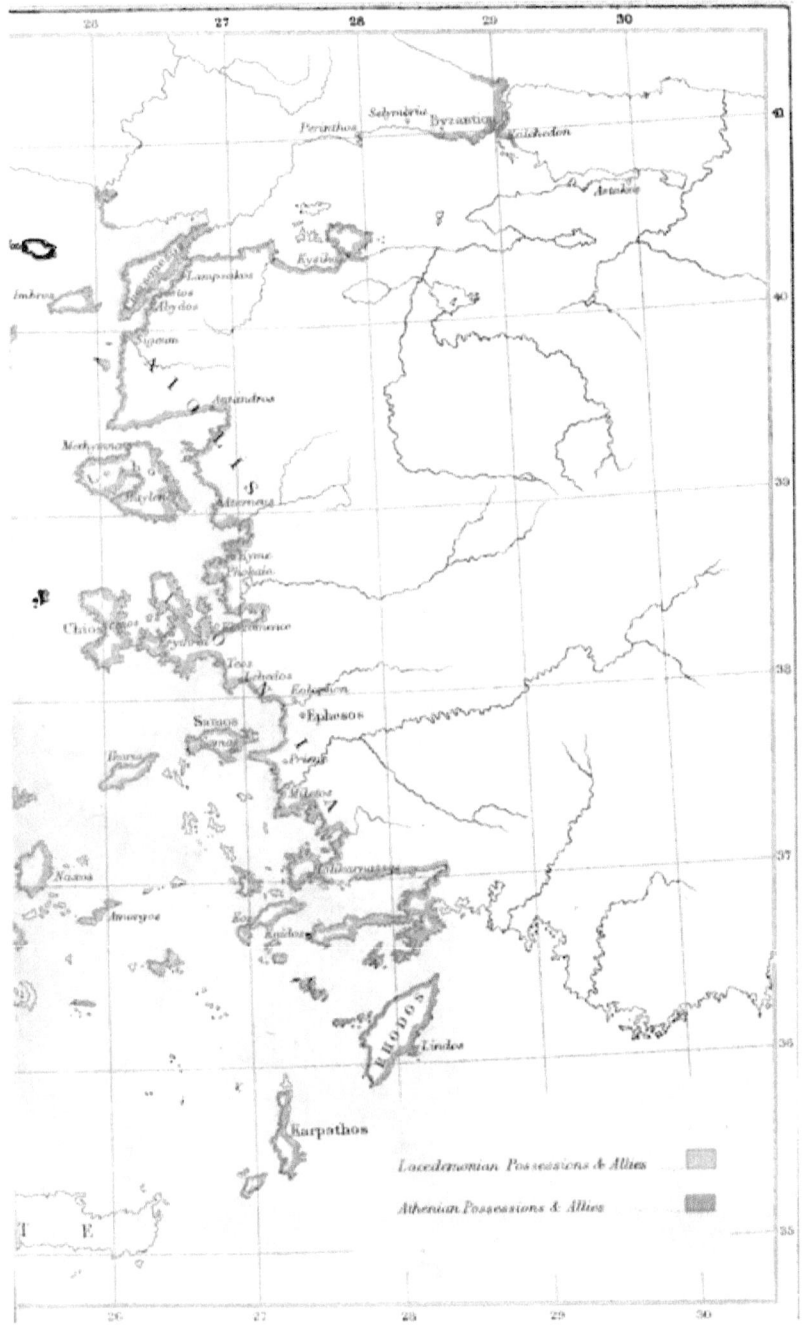

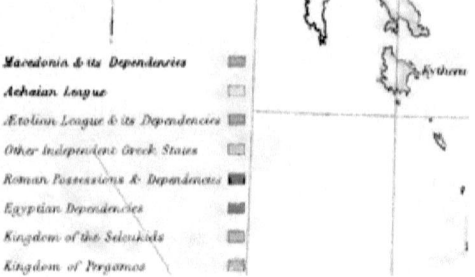

Macedonia & its Dependencies
Achaian League
Ætolian League & its Dependencies
Other Independent Greek States
Roman Possessions & Dependencies
Egyptian Dependencies
Kingdom of the Seleukids
Kingdom of Pergamos

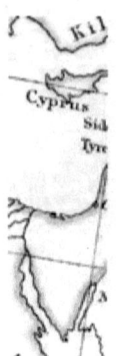

DOMINIONS AND DEPENDENCIES OF ALEXANDER c. B.C. 323.

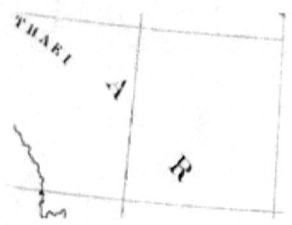

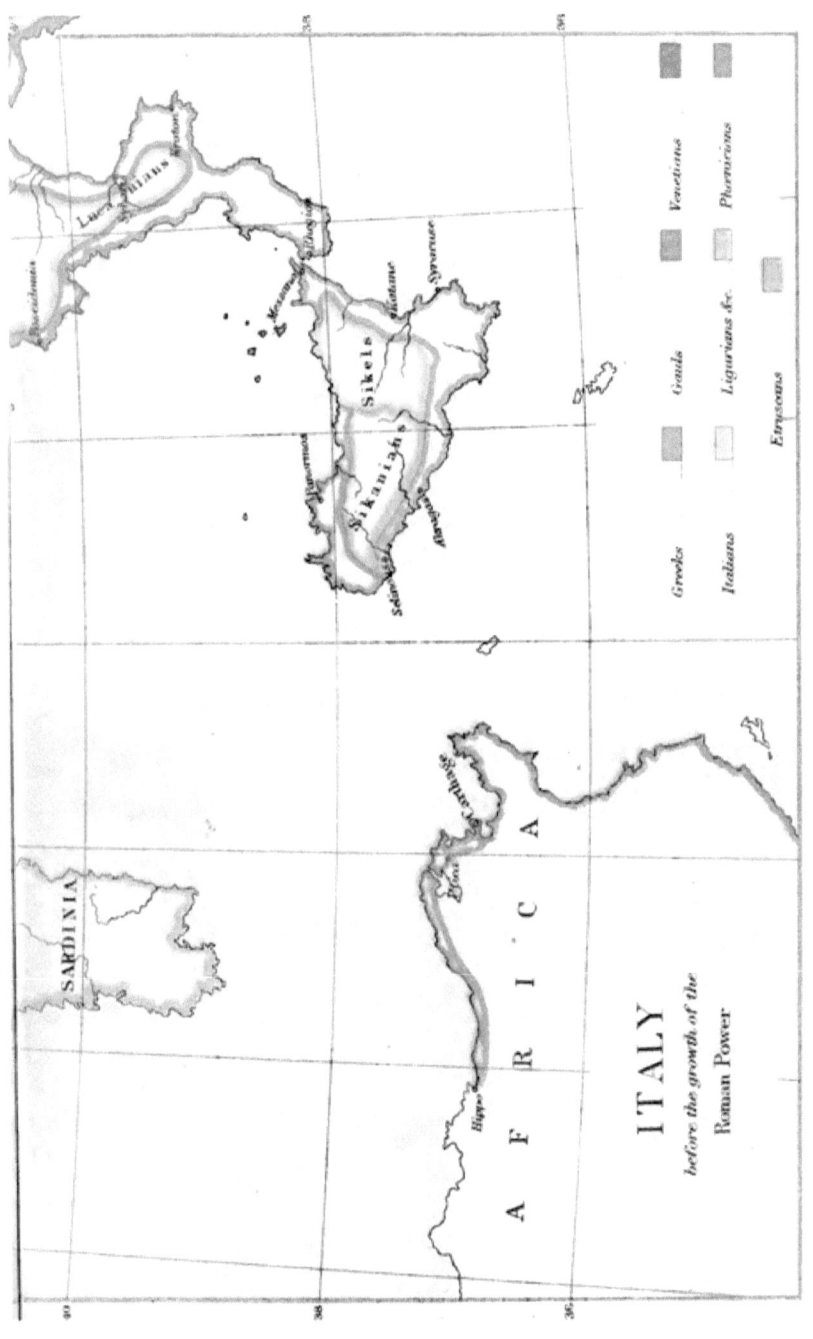

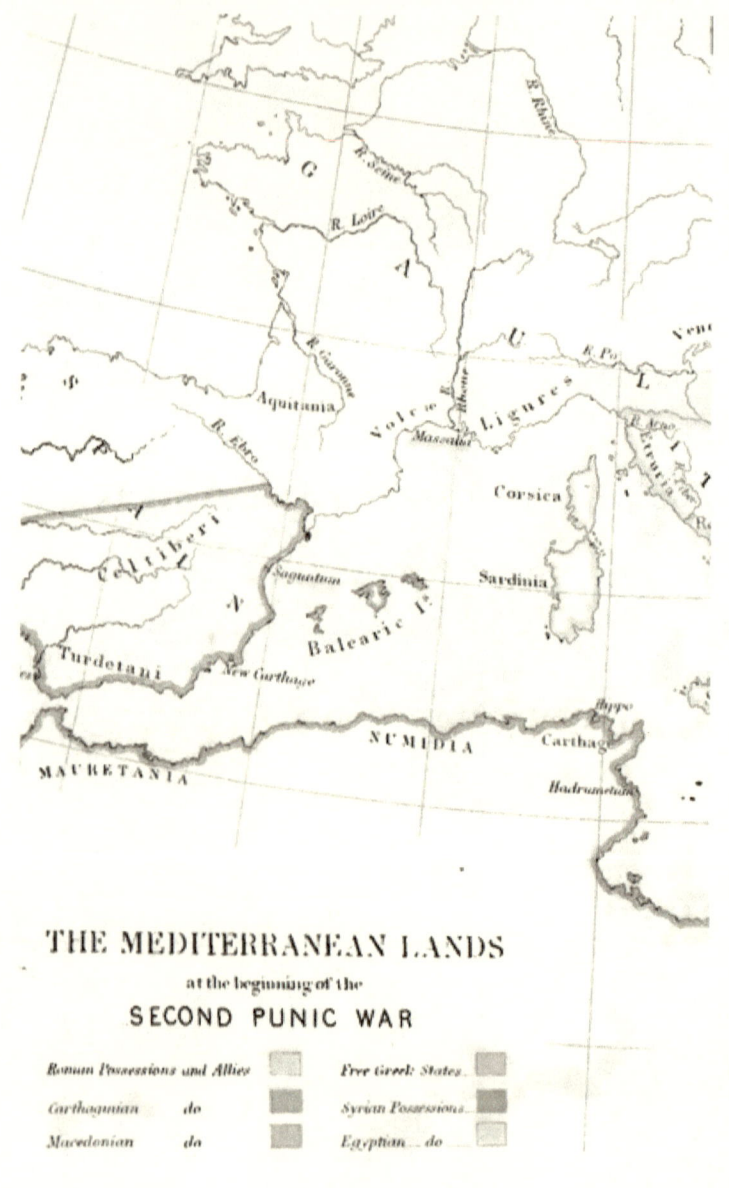

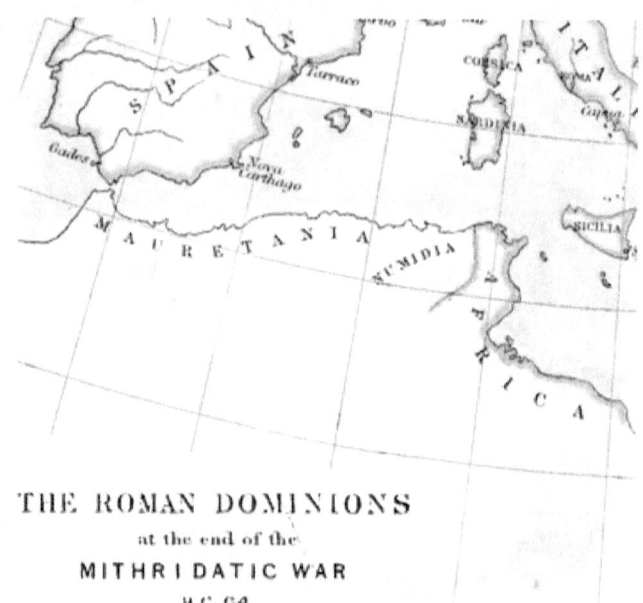

THE ROMAN DOMINIONS
at the end of the
MITHRIDATIC WAR
B.C. 64.

THE ROMAN EMPIRE
AT THE DEATH OF AUGUSTUS

A.D. 13.

THE ROMAN EMPIRE
UNDER TRAJAN
A.D. 117.

ROMAN EMPIRE
divided into
PREFECTURES

rks   CH
  ars   ZARS
g

GREATEST EXTENT
of the
SARACEN DOMINIONS

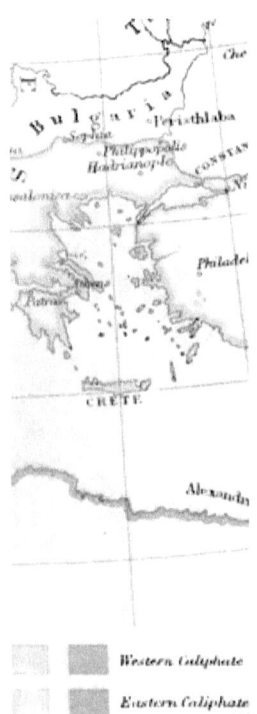

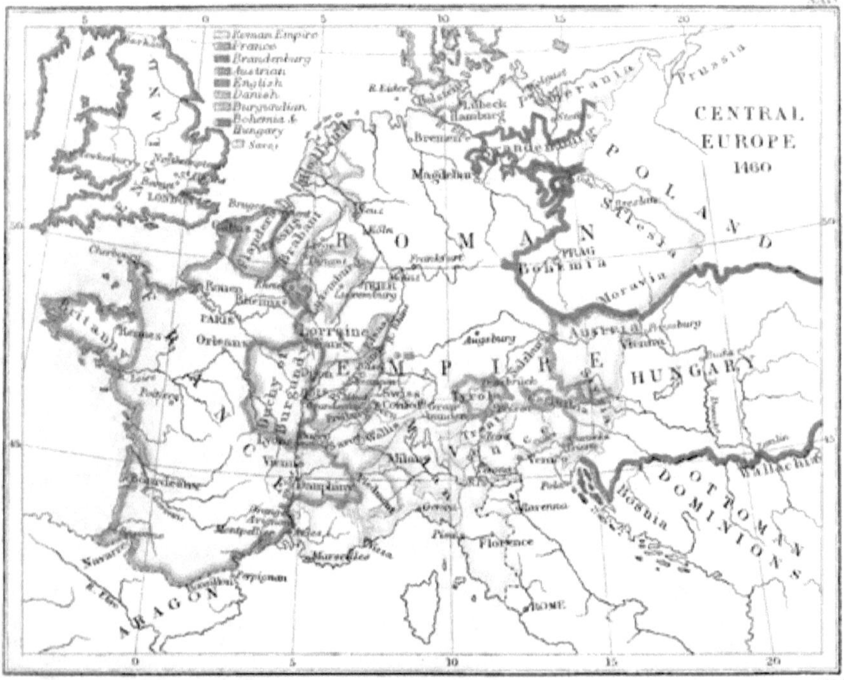

XXVIII

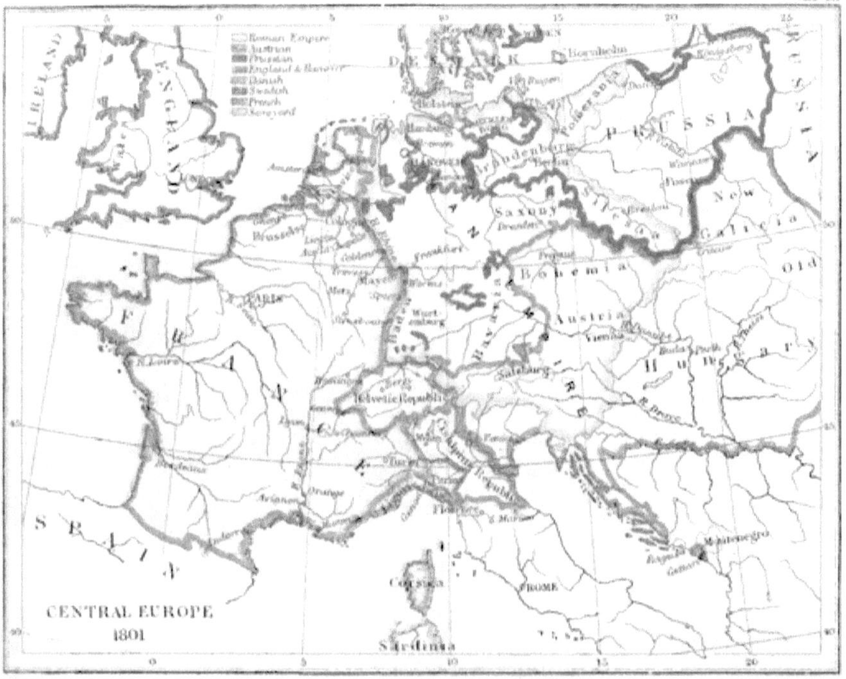
CENTRAL EUROPE
1801
Roman Empire
Austrian
Prussian
England & Hanover
Danish
Swedish
French
Savoyard
IRELAND
ENGLAND
DENMARK
Bornholm
Königsberg
RUSSIA
PRUSSIA
Pomerania
Brandenburg
Berlin
Silesia
New Galicia
Saxony
Dresden
Bohemia
Old
Brussels
Paris
FRANCE
R. Loire
Bordeaux
SPAIN
Helvetic Republic
Salzburg
Austria
Vienna
Hungary
Buda
Pesth
R. Drave
Montenegro
Florence
Corsica
ROME
Sardinia

XXIX

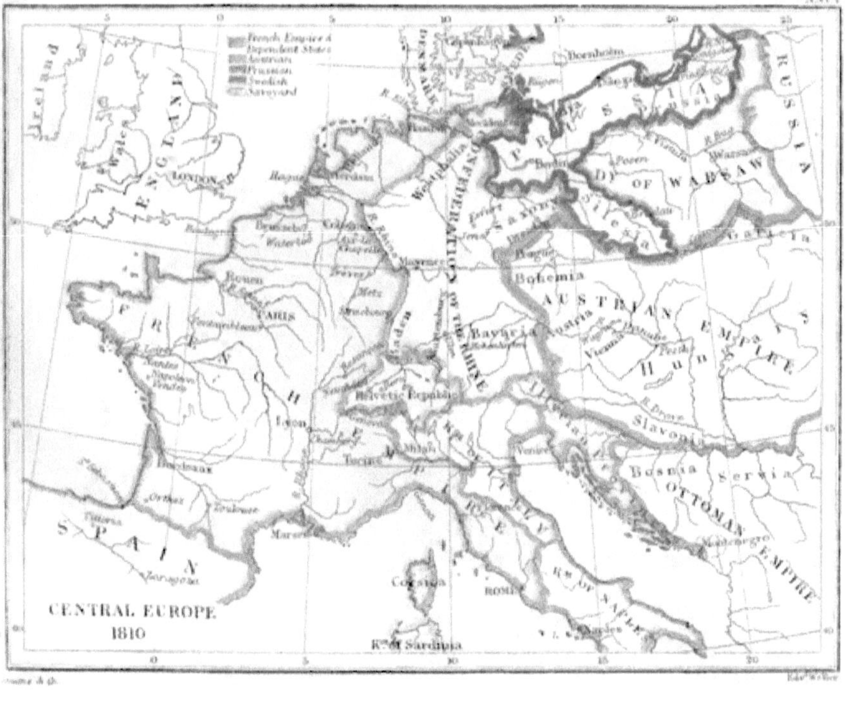
CENTRAL EUROPE
1810
French Empire & Dependent States
Austrian
Prussian
Swedish
Savoyard
Ireland
ENGLAND
Wales
LONDON
DENMARK
Bornholm
RUSSIA
PRUSSIA
Berlin
DY OF WARSAW
Posen
Silesia
Galicia
Westphalia
CONFEDERATION OF THE RHINE
Saxony
Bohemia
AUSTRIAN EMPIRE
Bavaria
Vienna
Hungary
Rouen
PARIS
FRANCE
R. Loire
Nantes
Bordeaux
Lyon
Helvetic Republic
Milan
Turin
Illyria
Slavonia
Bosnia
Servia
OTTOMAN EMPIRE
Montenegro
SPAIN
Corsica
ROME
Naples
Kdm. of Sardinia

CENTRAL EUROPE
1815

CENTRAL EUROPE
1860

CENTRAL
EUROPE
1871

BOUNDARY OF FRANCE
1555

BOUNDARY OF FRANCE
1715

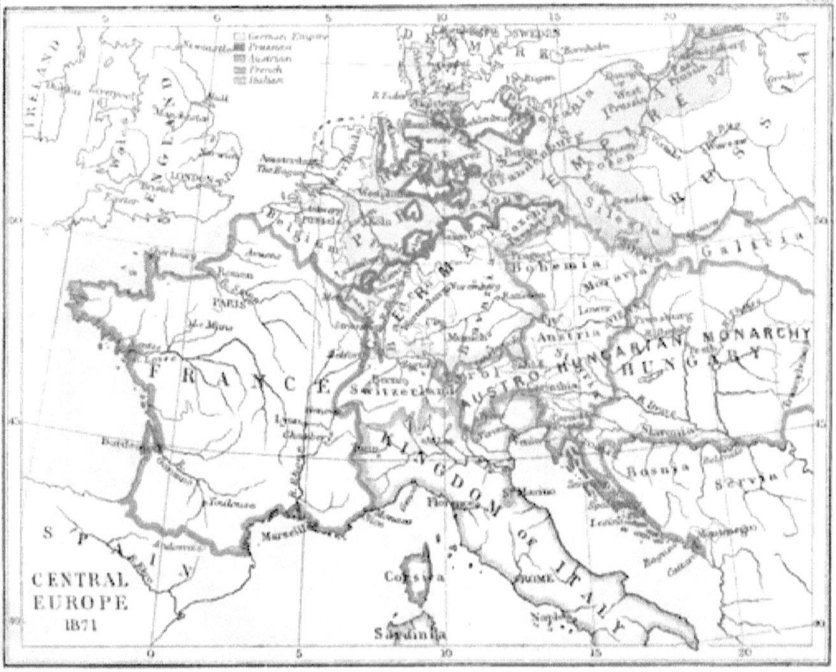

BOUNDARY OF FRANCE
1789

BOUNDARY OF FRANCE
1871

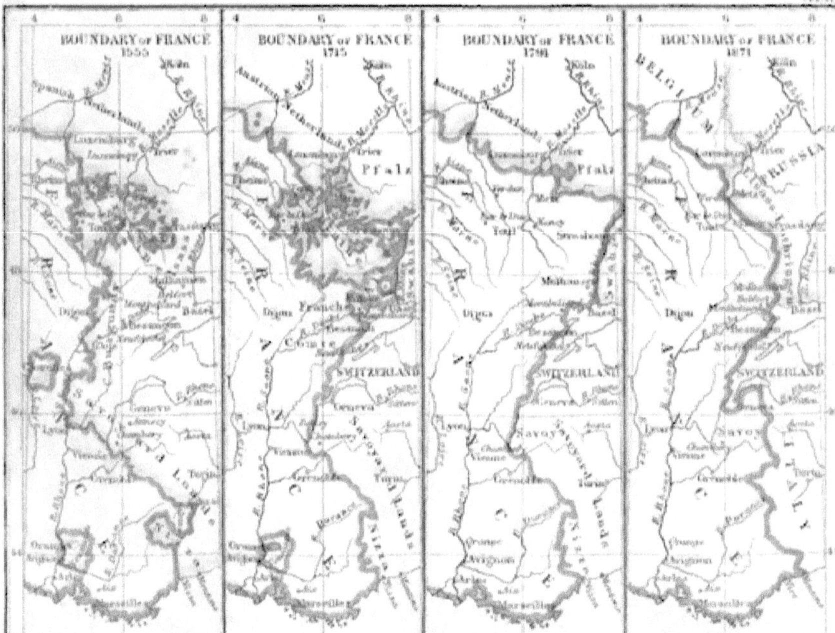

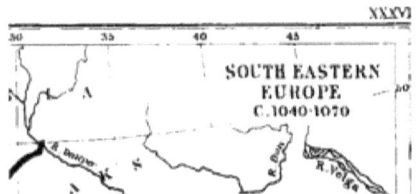

XLIV

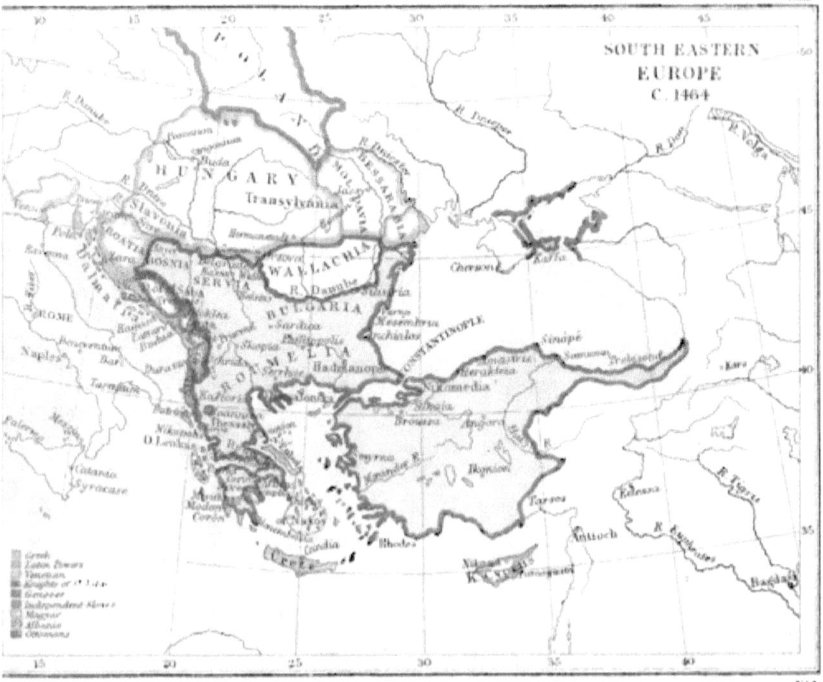

XLV

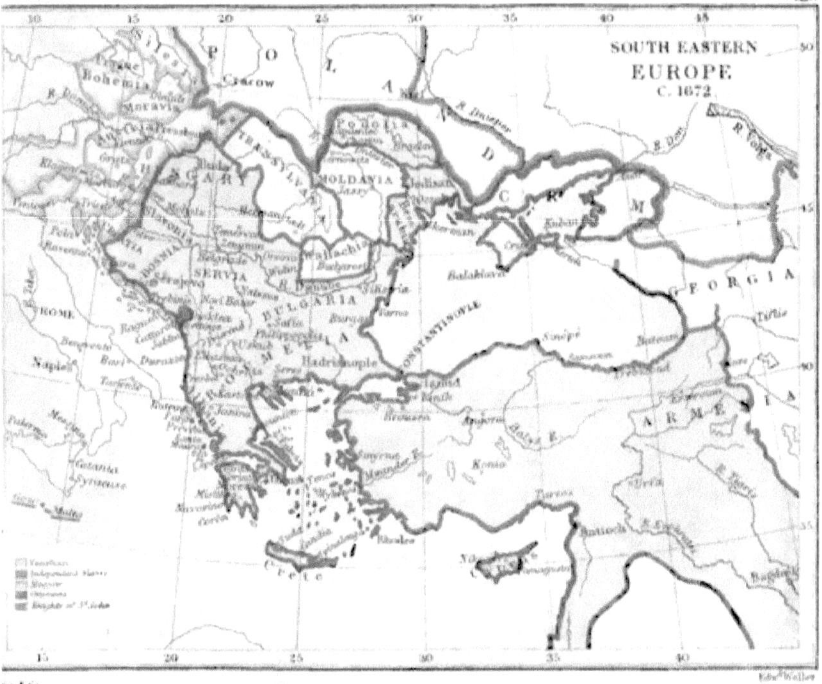

...ne & Co. Edwd Weller

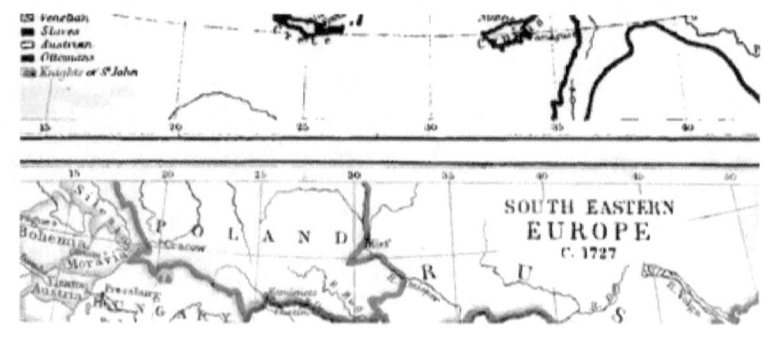

SOUTH EASTERN
EUROPE
C. 1727

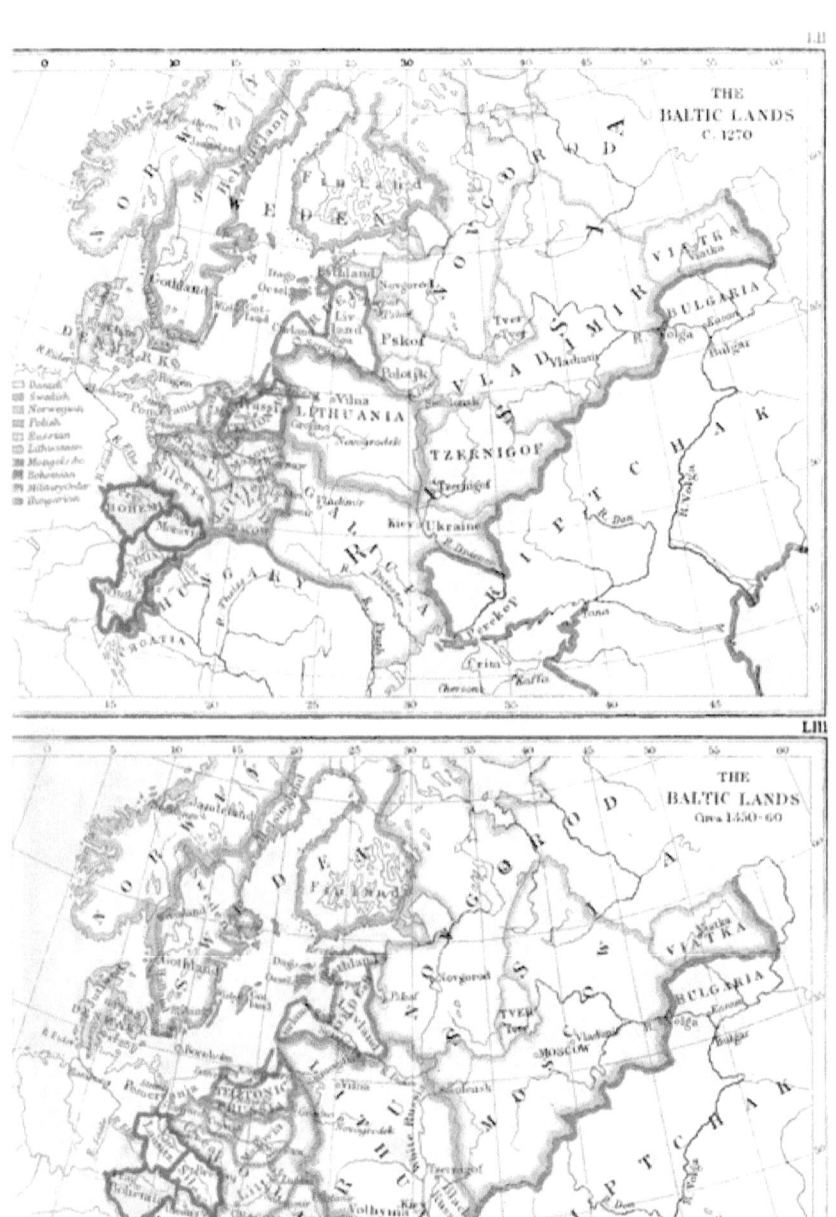

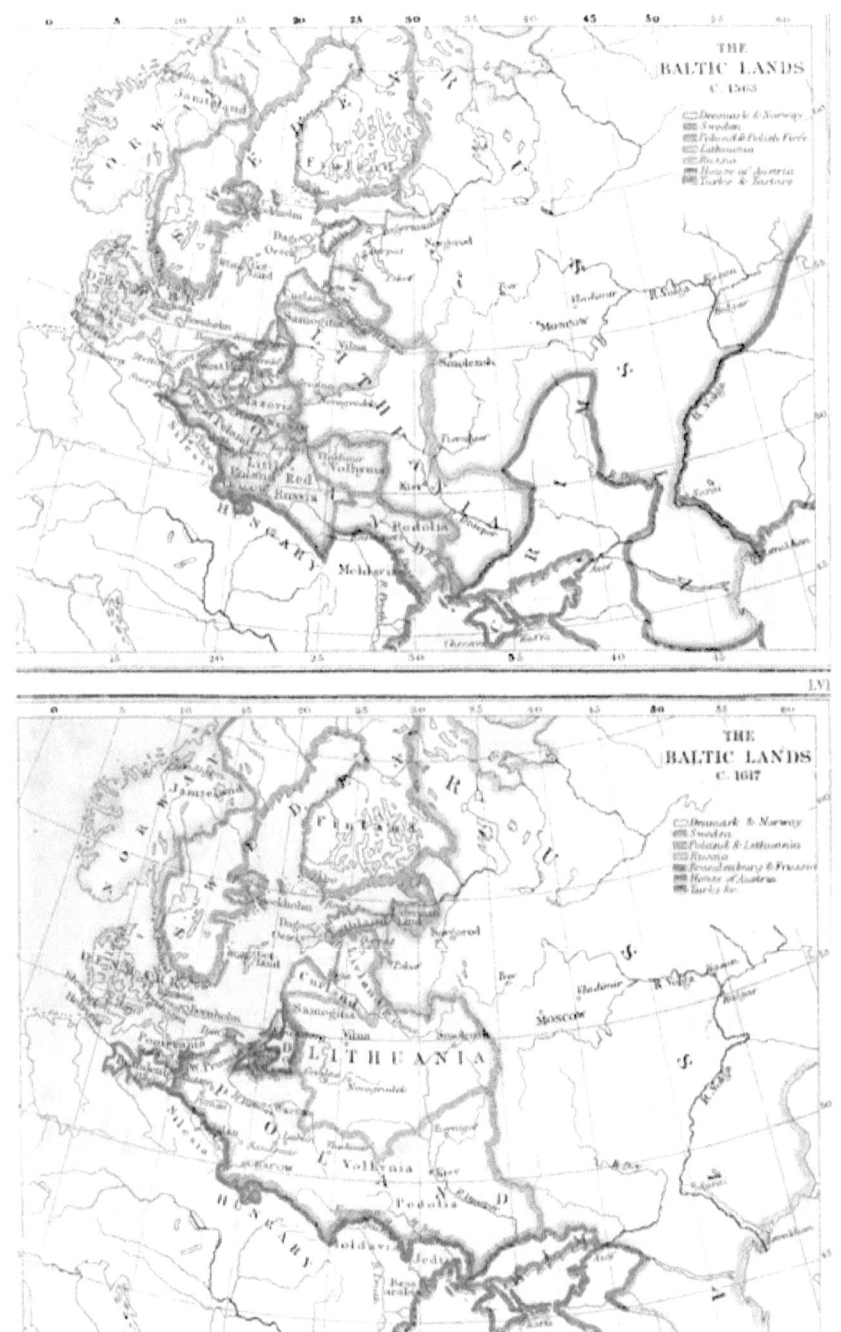

THE
BALTIC L.
C. 1772

☐ Denmark &
■ Sweden
■ Poland & L.
☐ Russia
■ Prussia
■ House of
■ Turks &c.

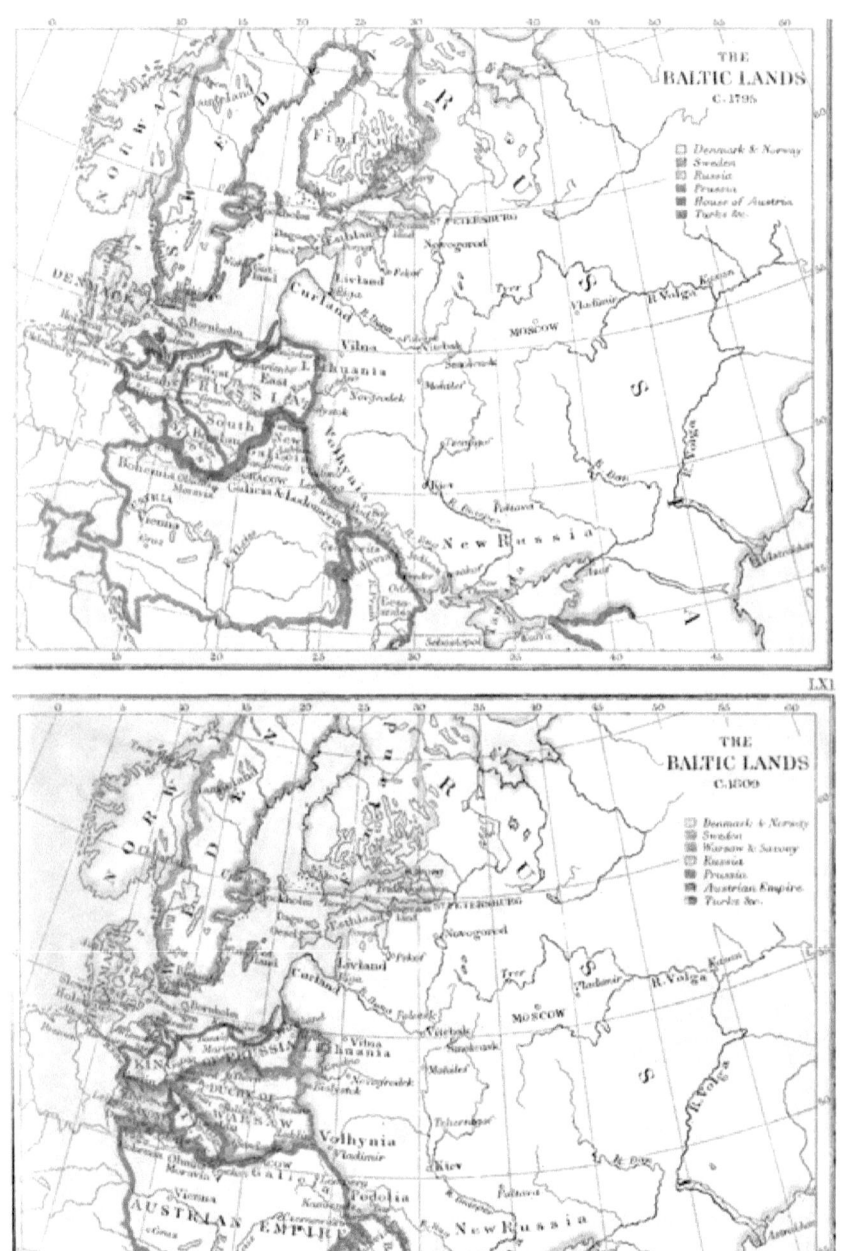

THE
SPANISH KINGDOMS
1030

THE
SPANISH KINGDOMS
1210

THE
SPANISH KINGDOMS
1360

Mussulmans
Navarre
Castile & Leon
France
Portugal
Aragon

THE
SPANISH KINGDOMS
and their European dependencies
under Charles the Fifth

Mussulmans
Navarre
Castile & Leon
France
Portugal

www.ingramcontent.com/pod-product-compliance
Lightning Source LLC
Chambersburg PA
CBHW020126170426
43199CB00009B/662